COPYRIGHT © 2014

All rights reserved.
No part of this publication
may be reproduced,
distributed or transmitted
in any form or by any means
including photocopying,
recording or other
electronic or mechanical
methods, without
the prior written
permission of the publisher,
except in the case
of brief quotations
embodied in critical reviews
and certain other
non commercial uses permitted
by copyright law.

I Spy
coloring book for Kids

This Book belongs to:

I SPY WITH MY LITTLE EYE SOMETHING STARTING WITH

It's an Apple

I SPY WITH MY LITTLE EYE SOMETHING STARTING WITH B

It's a Barrel

I SPY WITH MY LITTLE EYE SOMETHING STARTING WITH C

It's a Clover

I SPY WITH MY LITTLE EYE SOMETHING STARTING WITH D

It's a Drink

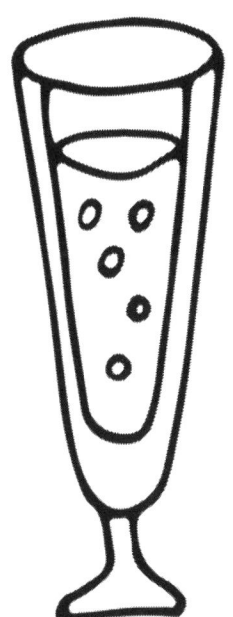

I SPY WITH MY LITTLE EYE SOMETHING STARTING WITH E

It's an Egg

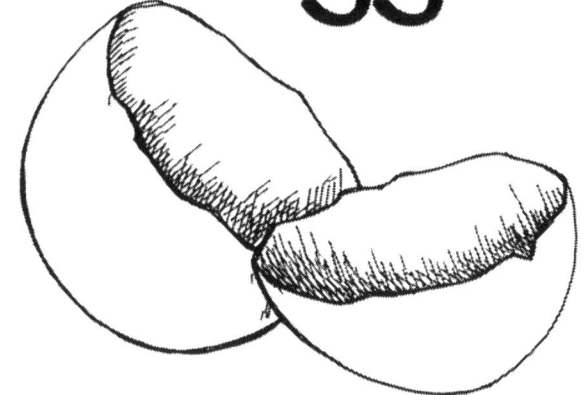

I SPY WITH MY LITTLE EYE SOMETHING STARTING WITH

It's a Flag

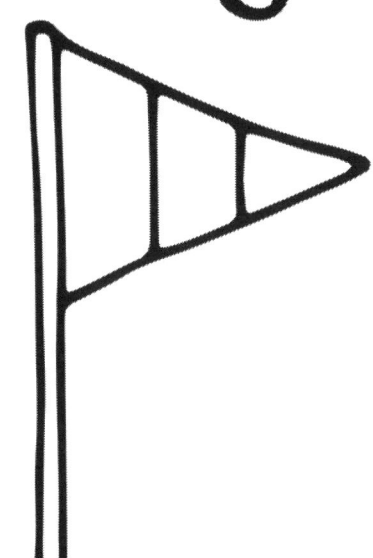

I SPY WITH MY LITTLE EYE SOMETHING STARTING WITH G

It's Gold

I SPY WITH MY LITTLE EYE SOMETHING STARTING WITH H

It's a Hat

I SPY WITH MY LITTLE EYE SOMETHING STARTING WITH

It's an Irish Flag

I SPY WITH MY LITTLE EYE SOMETHING STARTING WITH

It's a Jug

I SPY WITH MY LITTLE EYE SOMETHING STARTING WITH K

It's a Kite

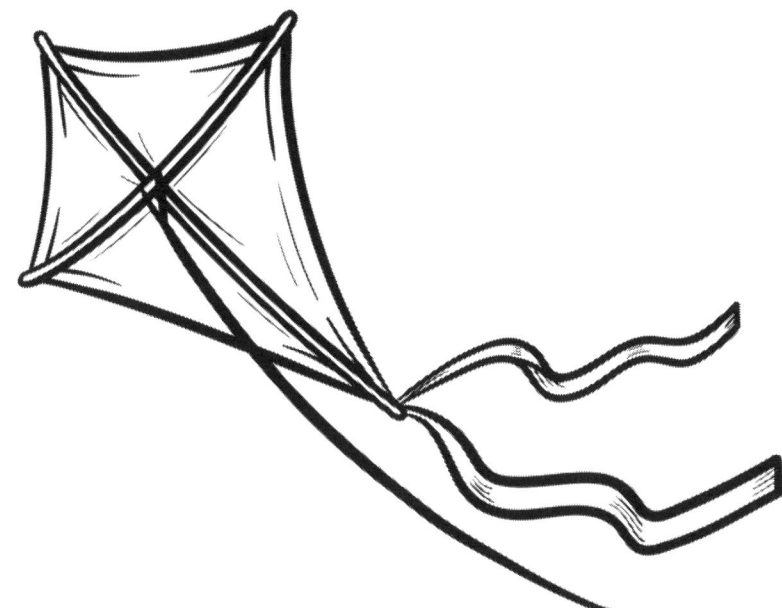

I SPY WITH MY LITTLE EYE SOMETHING STARTING WITH

It's a Leprechaun

I SPY WITH MY LITTLE EYE SOMETHING STARTING WITH M

It's a Mouse

I SPY WITH MY LITTLE EYE SOMETHING STARTING WITH N

4

I SPY WITH MY LITTLE EYE SOMETHING STARTING WITH

It's an Orange

I SPY WITH MY LITTLE EYE SOMETHING STARTING WITH

It's a Pot

I SPY WITH MY LITTLE EYE SOMETHING STARTING WITH

It's a Quill

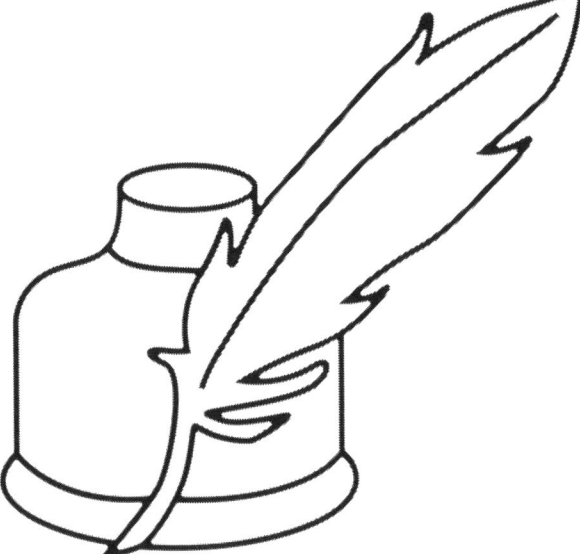

I SPY WITH MY LITTLE EYE SOMETHING STARTING WITH

It's a Rainbow

I SPY WITH MY LITTLE EYE SOMETHING STARTING WITH

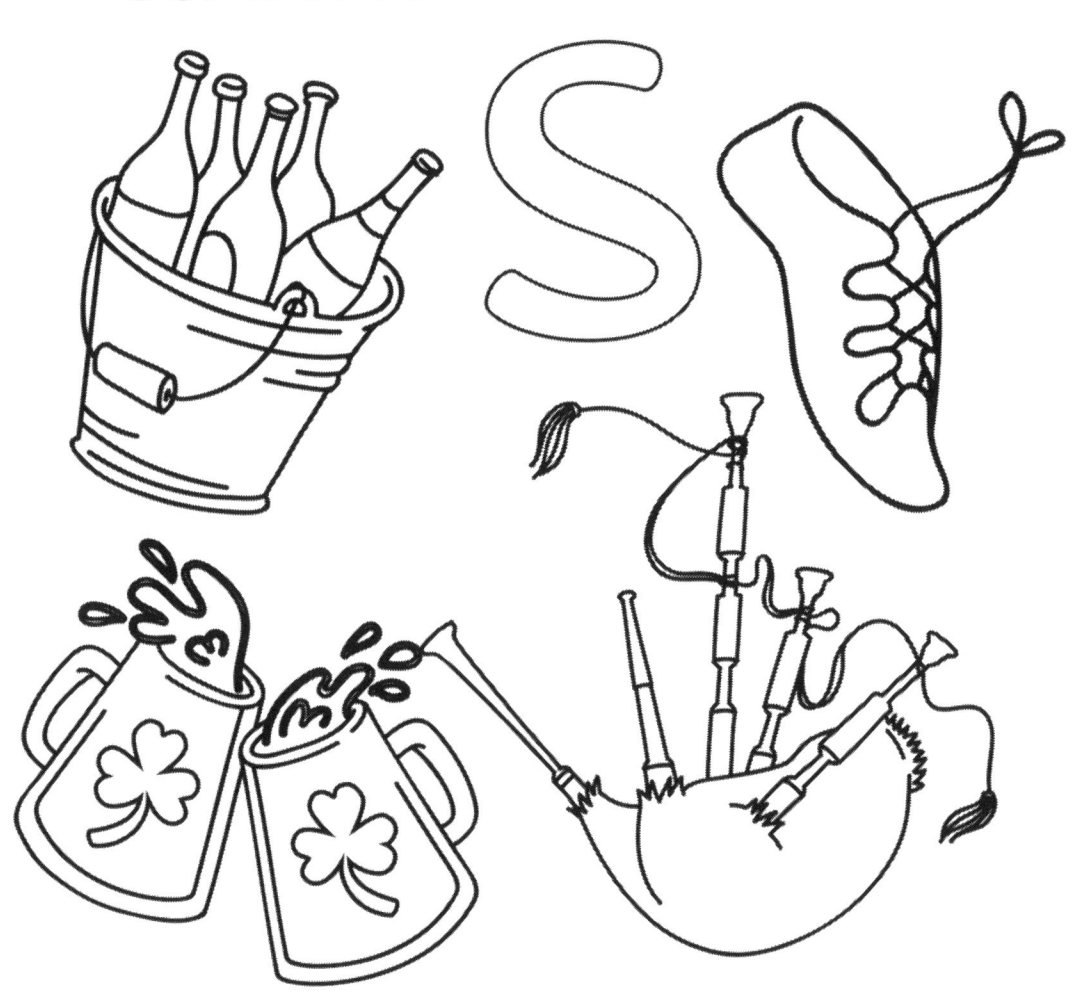

It's a Shoe

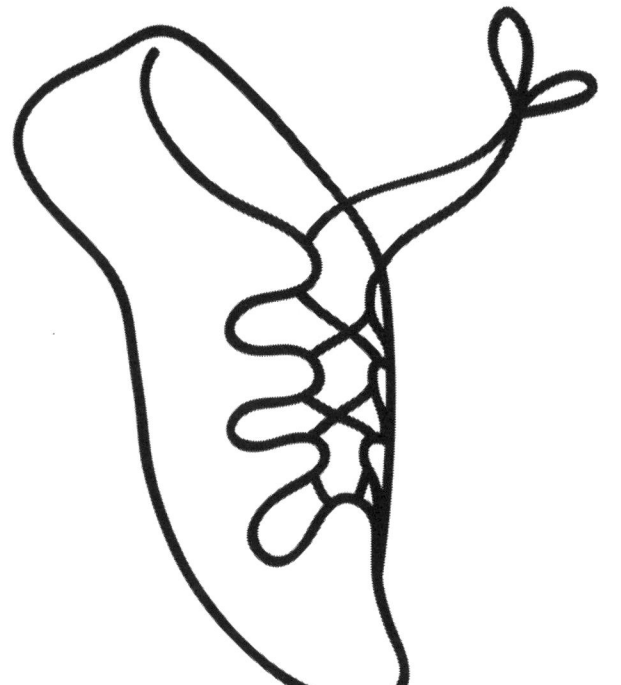

I SPY WITH MY LITTLE EYE SOMETHING STARTING WITH

It's a Tomato

I SPY WITH MY LITTLE EYE SOMETHING STARTING WITH

It's an Umbrella

I SPY WITH MY LITTLE EYE SOMETHING STARTING WITH

It's a Violin

I SPY WITH MY LITTLE EYE SOMETHING STARTING WITH W

It's a Whistle

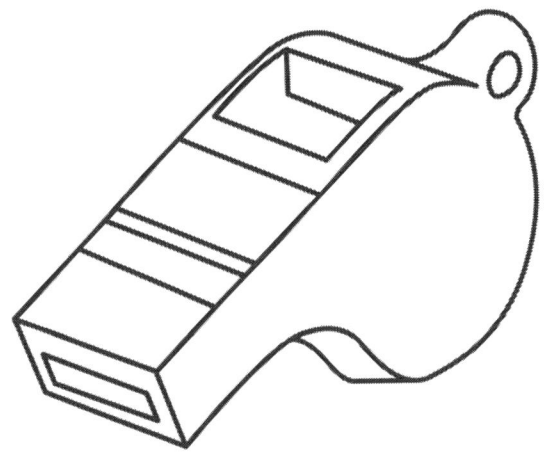

I SPY WITH MY LITTLE EYE SOMETHING STARTING WITH

It's an X-ray

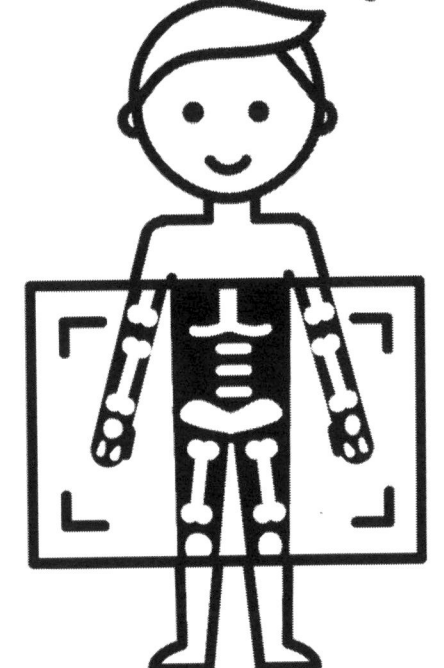

I SPY WITH MY LITTLE EYE SOMETHING STARTING WITH

It's Yarn

It's a Zeppelin

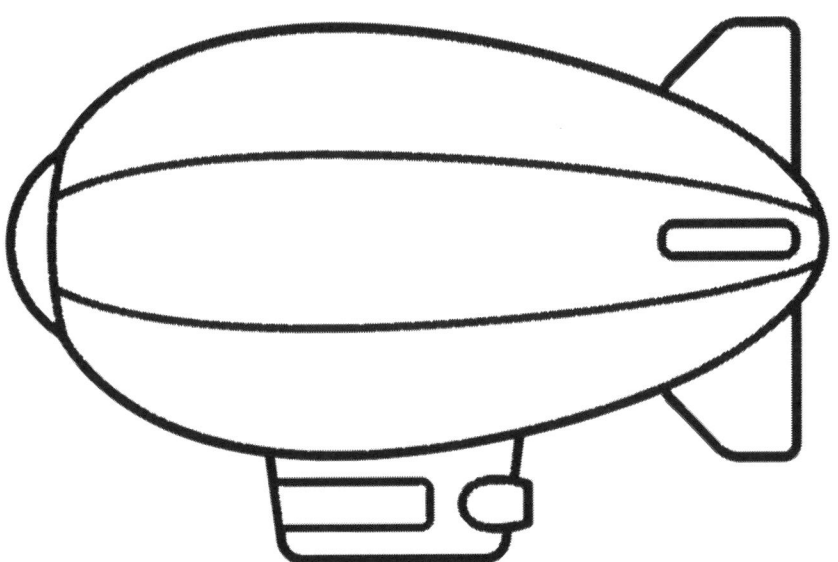

Made in the USA
Middletown, DE
02 March 2021